I AFFIRM ME

THE ABCs OF INSPIRATION FOR BLACK KIDS

Written by Nyasha Williams

Illustrated by Sóf'ya Glushkó

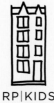

RP|KIDS

PHILADELPHIA

Mention of names in this book does not imply
that those individuals have endorsed the book, author, or publisher.

Running Press Kids
Hachette Book Group
1290 Avenue of the Americas, New York, NY 10104
www.runningpress.com/rpkids
@RP_Kids

Printed in China

First Edition: May 2021

Published by Running Press Kids, an imprint of Perseus Books, LLC,
a subsidiary of Hachette Book Group, Inc. The Running Press Kids
name and logo is a trademark of the Hachette Book Group.

The Hachette Speakers Bureau provides a wide range
of authors for speaking events. To find out more, go to
www.hachettespeakersbureau.com or call (866) 376-6591.

The publisher is not responsible for websites (or their content)
that are not owned by the publisher.

Print book cover and interior design by Frances J. Soo Ping Chow.
Illustration by Sóf'ya Glushkó

Library of Congress Cataloging-in-Publication Data
has been applied for.

ISBNs: 978-0-7624-7560-5 (hardcover), 978-0-7624-7559-9 (ebook),
978-0-7624-7565-0 (ebook), 978-0-7624-7566-7 (ebook)

APS

10 9 8 7 6 5 4 3 2 1

I dedicate this book to all Black children
to remind them of their worth.
You are irreplaceable, needed, and beloved.
You are enough. Your life matters.

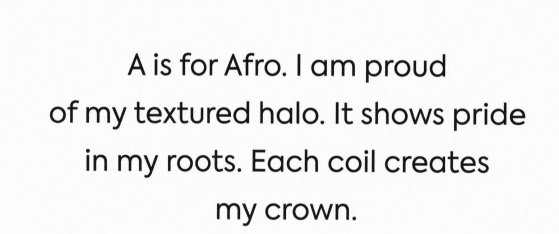

A is for Afro. I am proud
of my textured halo. It shows pride
in my roots. Each coil creates
my crown.

B is for Belong. I have value.
I add value to the world. The world
would not be the same without me.
My opinion matters.

Cc

C is for Challenge. I am ready
for today! I breathe in happiness and
release worry. I face my fears
and will overcome them. Today,
I will take action.

D is for Dreams. I am fully capable of achieving my dreams. I am surrounded by love and support for my dreams. I dare to follow my dreams. I am my ancestors' wildest dreams.

E is for Energy. I am ready to begin the day. My spirit is centered in love. I empower others with positive energy.

Ff

F is for Freedom. I am free to
become anyone I choose. I am here
on Earth to flourish and grow. I work
toward helping all people gain
freedom and bettering our world for
future generations.

Gg

G is for Global. I am part of a nurturing and amazing tribe of people. I am in harmony with my brothers and sisters. I am part of a global community.

H is for HBCU. My teachers know my worth and encourage my growth. I apply myself daily. I feed my mind with skills and experiences to thrive within my community, country, and world.

Ii

I is for Invention. I use the everyday
world all around to inspire me
creatively. I am always thinking
of new things to try.

J is for Justice. I live my truth every day.
I am enough. I am worthy. I take
action toward creating a just world.

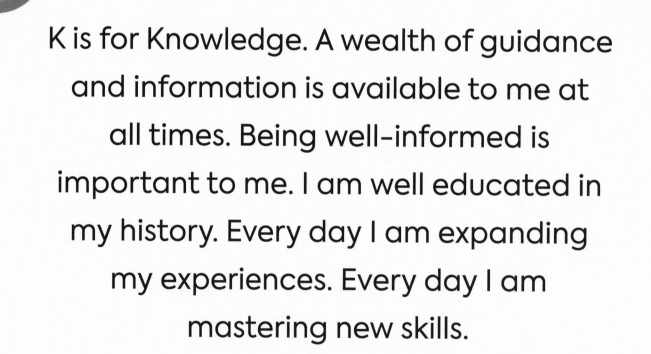

K is for Knowledge. A wealth of guidance and information is available to me at all times. Being well-informed is important to me. I am well educated in my history. Every day I am expanding my experiences. Every day I am mastering new skills.

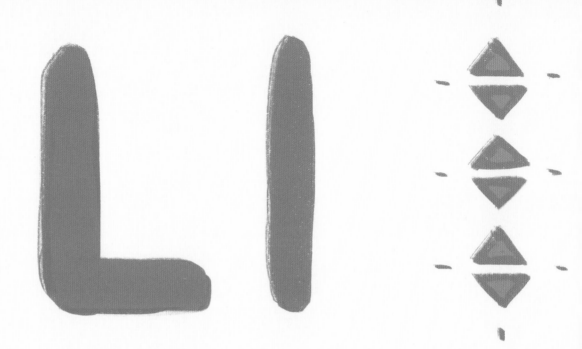

L is for Leader. I am a role model for others. I listen and learn. I have the confidence to stand up for myself because what I say matters.

M is for Mindfulness. I am mindful at all times and will live within each moment. I will be here, now.

N is for Natural. I love myself fully
and deeply. I radiate confidence,
self-respect, and inner harmony.
I am a diamond already.

O is for Optimistic. I am not perfect
and will make mistakes, but I will
always forgive myself as long as
I continue to learn.

P is for Pride. I am proud of
who I am and my accomplishments
so far. I give myself permission
to shine. I honor my background,
history, and experience.

Q is for Question. I will ask questions, seeking answers. I will ask questions when there is something I do not understand.

R is for Rally. I know when I lift another,
I am raised, too. I am working to build
a brighter future for all. Love flows
in and around my community.

S is for Spirituality. I am spiritually taught, trained, and advised, encouraged in all that I say, think, or do. I am enveloped by the Spirit. I am treasured, nourished, and loved.

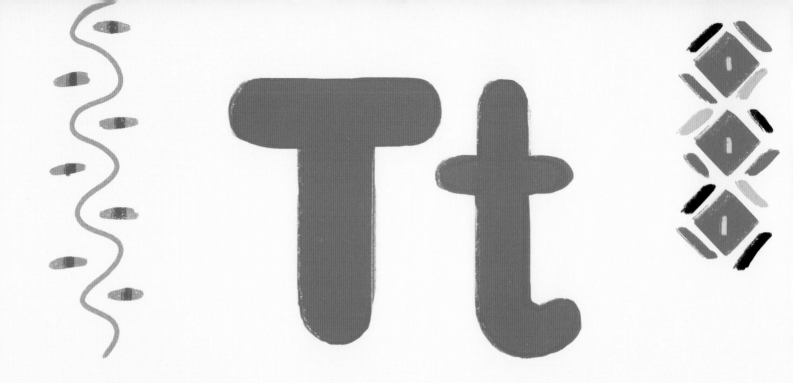

T is for Travel. I will become a globetrotter. I am inquisitive and adventurous. I go on journeys that lead to inviting locations and connect me to remarkable people.

U is for Unity. I surround myself with love and light. I care about what is going on in the world. I am one with the universe. I am whole. I am peace.

V is for Vision. I see. I create.
It becomes. I see myself and everything
around me clearly.

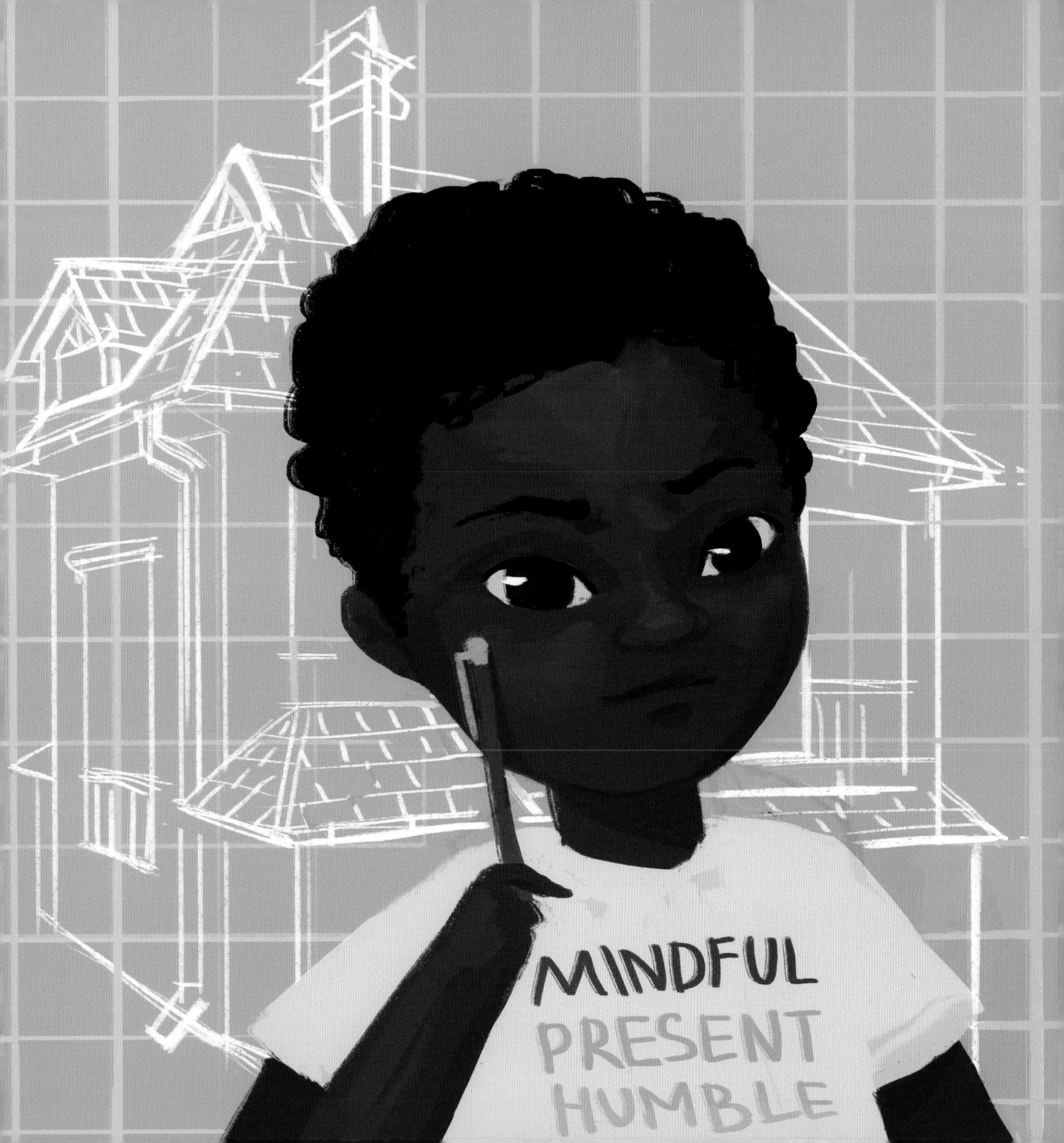
MINDFUL
PRESENT
HUMBLE

W is for Wisdom. I use my common
sense to discern and direct my path.
I think before I react.

X is for eXcellent. I can. I will.
I am constantly working on myself.
I radiate growth. I attract new
and healthy experiences.

Y is for Youth. I have the power to create change. I am proud to be part of the future generation. I love and care for the Earth as the Earth loves and cares for me.

Z is for Zen. I center my mind.
I ready my body. I nourish my spirit.